THE 10

Greatest
Movies from Books

Carol Drake

Series Editor
Jeffrey D. Wilhelm

Much thought, debate, and research went into choosing and ranking the 10 items in each book in this series. We realize that everyone has his or her own opinion of what is most significant, revolutionary, amazing, deadly, and so on. As you read, you may agree with our choices, or you may be surprised — and that's the way it should be!

Franklin Watts®

an imprint of

SCHOLASTIC

www.scholastic.com/librarypublishing

A Rubicon book published in association with Scholastic Inc.

SCHOLASTIC and associated logos and designs are trademarks and/or registered trademarks of Scholastic Inc.

Rubicon © 2007 Rubicon Publishing Inc.
www.rubiconpublishing.com

 is a trademark of The 10 Books

Associate Publishers: Kim Koh, Miriam Bardswich
Project Editor: Amy Land
Editor: Caitlin Drake
Creative Director: Jennifer Drew
Project Manager/Designer: Jeanette MacLean
Graphic Designer: Victoria Cigan

The publisher gratefully acknowledges the following for permission to reprint copyrighted material in this book.

Every reasonable effort has been made to trace the owners of copyrighted material and to make due acknowledgment. Any errors or omissions drawn to our attention will be gladly rectified in future editions.

"*Crouching Tiger, Hidden Dragon*" (excerpt) by Elvis Mitchell, from *The New York Times*, October 9, 2000. Used with permission.

"He's Green and Groovy, Baby" (excerpt) by Jeanne Wolf, from "The Shrek Who Shagged Me" in *TV Guide Insider*, May 18, 2001. Used with permission.

"The Next Reel: Interview with Peter Jackson and Philippa Boyens" (excerpt) by Nina Rehfeld, December 18, 2002. Used with permission.

Cover: *The Lord of the Rings* poster artwork–Photo by New Line Cinema/ KPA-ZUMA/KEYSTONE Press. (©) Copyright 2002 by New Line Cinema; all other images–Shutterstock

Library and Archives Canada Cataloguing in Publication

Drake, Carol
  The 10 greatest movies from books / Carol Drake.

Includes index.
ISBN 978-1-55448-463-8

  1. Readers (Elementary) 2. Readers—Motion pictures.
I. Title. II. Title: Ten greatest movies from books.

PE1117.D734 2007a   428.6   C2007-902007-0

1 2 3 4 5 6 7 8 9 10   10   16 15 14 13 12 11 10 09 08 07

Printed in Singapore

Contents

6

18

26

Watched a Good Book Lately?

Pssst ... Want the secret recipe for making a hit film? Sorry, there are no guarantees in Hollywood, baby. Movies with million-dollar budgets can become huge bombs and unknown independent films can become mega-blockbusters.

That is one of the reasons why movie producers pay millions of dollars to secure film rights to books. But not all books — including best sellers — can be transformed into successful movies. First, you need a book with a gripping story, dramatic plot, appealing characters, and exciting setting. Then, you need a movie producer who can recognize these elements in a book. The producer then has to find a skilled screenwriter who can turn the book into a successful screenplay.

When ranking the 10 best movies from books, we considered many things. These films have gone from the page to the screen with great success. They are watched over and over again — in the movie theater and the home theater. Some will make you laugh yourself silly. Others might make you scared or sad. A few of them have special effects that will blow your mind. These films have endured because they expressed a powerful message that moved audiences and changed our way of life.

So, now it's time to make some popcorn, settle down on the couch, and ask the following question ...

What is the greatest movie based on a book?

Michelle Yeoh (right) and Zhang Ziyi in Crouching Tiger, Hidden Dragon

WHEN: Producer/director Ang Lee surprised the world with this amazing production in 2000.

BASED ON: *Crouching Tiger, Hidden Dragon,* by Wang Du Lu (early 1940s)

WHY IT'S COOL: Spectacular fight sequences, sensitive acting, and stirring music combine to create an action movie that also packs an emotional punch.

"Violent." "Plotless." "Just plain silly." Kung fu movies are usually slammed by the critics, but *Crouching Tiger, Hidden Dragon* delivers a lethal karate chop to all the haters!

Based on a book of the same title written by Wang Du Lu, this movie is so powerful that you can't take your eyes off it. Who would believe that a martial arts movie could also be enjoyed by film snobs? Filmed entirely in the city of Beijing and the Chinese countryside, the movie brings the magnificent scenery of China to our North American doorsteps.

The astounding ballet of martial arts moves accompanied by the haunting cello music of Yo-Yo Ma make us believe that men can fly — and that women can fly even higher!

But wait — *Crouching Tiger, Hidden Dragon* isn't only about combat skills. It's also a tale of triumph, tragedy, and love. Ultimately, it is about the hidden and powerful dragon within all of us.

CROUCHING TIGER, HIDDEN DRAGON

WHAT'S THE STORY?

Chow Yun Fat stars as Li Mu Bai who wants to hang up his sword and live happily ever after with his true love, Yu Shu Lien. But Li has two "small" problems: (1) their love must be secret; and (2) his sword, Green Destiny, needs to be protected. Green Destiny is a 400-year-old magical sword — and in the wrong hands, it can be very dangerous!

Jen is a headstrong young woman (Jen's Chinese name means "pampered dragon"). She rebels against an aristocratic family by falling in love with an outlaw. Jen manages to steal Green Destiny, which triggers a tragic series of events.

CONFLICT ZONE

Everyone gets into the action as combat skill defies traditional male/female roles. But the real conflict isn't in the fight sequences — it's the inner struggle within each of the characters!

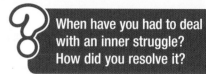

? When have you had to deal with an inner struggle? How did you resolve it?

FROM PAGE TO SCREEN

Wang Du Lu wrote the novel *Crouching Tiger, Hidden Dragon* in Chinese in the early 1940s. It was the fourth book in his Crane-Iron pentalogy. Over 60 years later, Andy Seto used the original text to illustrate a 13-volume graphic novel!

aristocratic: *upper class*
pentalogy: *series of five books*

Quick Fact
In Chinese mythology the phrase "crouching tiger, hidden dragon" means hiding your strength from others.

Zhang Ziyi as Jen in Crouching Tiger, Hidden Dragon

Quick Fact
With its exotic setting and fabulous cinematography and music, it's hard to believe that this film had a budget of only $15 million! Despite its low budget, *Crouching Tiger* grossed $128 million in U.S. box offices alone!

cinematography: *art of shooting movies*

Crouching Tiger, Hidden Dragon

By Elvis Mitchell

A newspaper review from *The New York Times*, October 9, 2000

In [director] Ang Lee's soulful action film, *Crouching Tiger, Hidden Dragon*, Chow Yun Fat strides onto the screen proud, erect, and easy. ... His witty reserve is used beautifully here and the picture is more fun than it has a right to be.

Any collaboration featuring Mr. Lee, Mr. Chow, Michelle Yeoh, Yo-Yo Ma, and the wizard martial arts choreographer Yuen Wo-Ping is bound to spike expectations through the roof, as well as start more than a few hands scratching heads in confusion. What are these guys doing working together? They're applying their specialties to a Hong Kong action movie that rings with confidence and is being shown tonight as the closing film of the New York Film Festival.

Mr. Lee takes the action form, which often attacks the screen with energy and movement, and creates a placid surface that offers a new perspective and a spirituality not normally found in these pictures. In terms of action, nothing much takes place for the first 10 minutes. That's so he can set up the incredibly complicated plot, which has as much romance, intrigue, free-wheeling action — and rousing silliness — as any five Hong Kong throw-down fests. ... Mr. Lee puts things together artfully and stages this movie like a comedy of manners. ...

Mr. Lee has found a way to make even the action feel poetic and spiritual, while sparked by a high adrenaline content. The first fight scene, which brings all the principals together, will make you want to applaud. ...

reserve: *calmness*

Crouching Tiger, Hidden Dragon gives us a better understanding of honor, loyalty, and tradition. Why are these values important?

Quick Fact

In 2005, Ang Lee was the first Asian to win the Academy Award for Best Director. In most movies, the director tells his or her actors and crew how to make the film look and sound exactly the way he or she had imagined it.

The Expert Says...

" *Crouching Tiger, Hidden Dragon* is an astonishingly beautiful film. It's like a Chinese painting. It's like a musical. It's an adult fairy tale.

— Michelle Yeoh, *Crouching Tiger, Hidden Dragon* actress in the role of Yu Shu Lien

Take Note

Crouching Tiger, Hidden Dragon leaped over boundaries and introduced martial arts to mainstream audiences. That giant leap also landed it at #10 on our list!
• What qualities does *Crouching Tiger* have that make it the best of its genre and interesting to a wide range of viewers? Does it have enough appeal to rank higher on our list?

5   4   3   2   1

Actors Ralph Macchio, Matt Dillon, and C. Thomas Howell

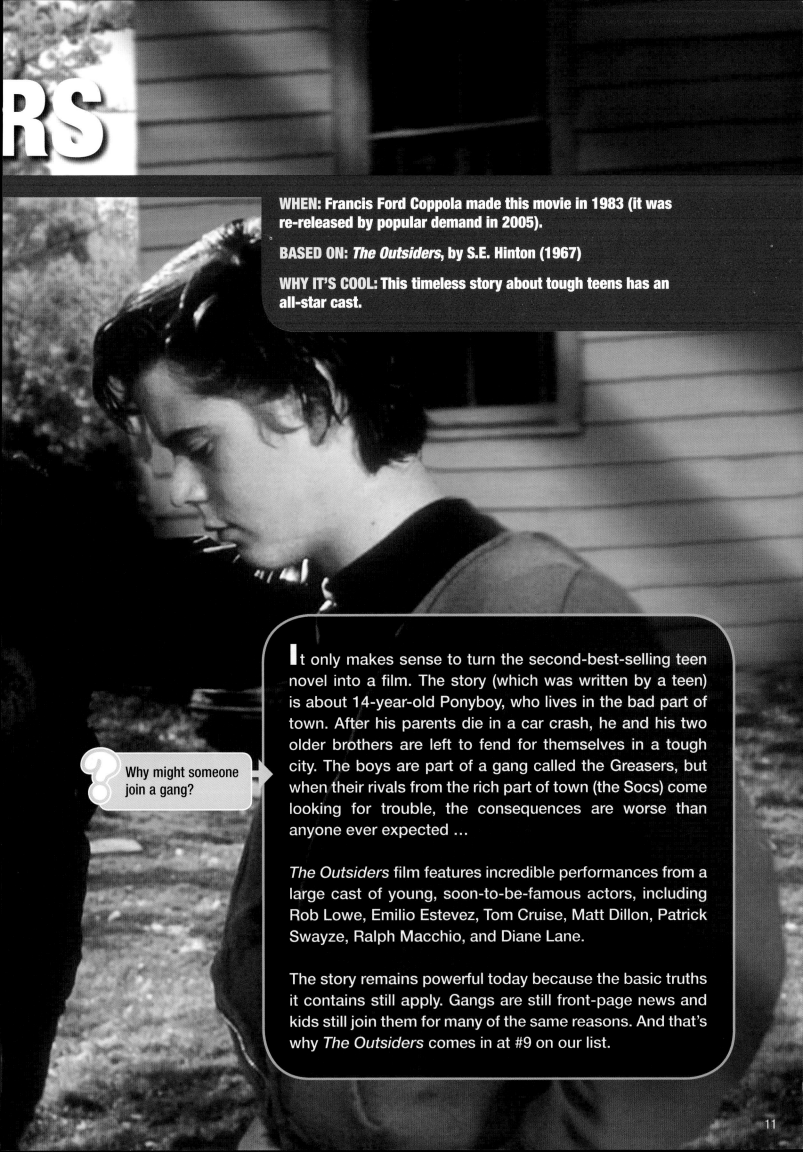

RS

WHEN: Francis Ford Coppola made this movie in 1983 (it was re-released by popular demand in 2005).

BASED ON: *The Outsiders*, by S.E. Hinton (1967)

WHY IT'S COOL: This timeless story about tough teens has an all-star cast.

Why might someone join a gang?

It only makes sense to turn the second-best-selling teen novel into a film. The story (which was written by a teen) is about 14-year-old Ponyboy, who lives in the bad part of town. After his parents die in a car crash, he and his two older brothers are left to fend for themselves in a tough city. The boys are part of a gang called the Greasers, but when their rivals from the rich part of town (the Socs) come looking for trouble, the consequences are worse than anyone ever expected ...

The Outsiders film features incredible performances from a large cast of young, soon-to-be-famous actors, including Rob Lowe, Emilio Estevez, Tom Cruise, Matt Dillon, Patrick Swayze, Ralph Macchio, and Diane Lane.

The story remains powerful today because the basic truths it contains still apply. Gangs are still front-page news and kids still join them for many of the same reasons. And that's why *The Outsiders* comes in at #9 on our list.

THE OUTSIDERS

WHAT'S THE STORY?

One night after a movie, Ponyboy and Johnny make friends with Cherry and Marcia who are members of the Socs (the preppy crowd). This infuriates the girls' boyfriends, who are also Socs. They attack Ponyboy and attempt to drown him. This clash sets off a complicated chain of events that ultimately ends in disaster.

CONFLICT ZONE

A shoving match between the "haves" and the "have-nots" gets out of hand and turns into terrible warfare. As with most wars, there are many casualties and few real winners. The challenge is to somehow "stay gold."

FROM PAGE TO SCREEN

S.E. Hinton wrote *The Outsiders* in 1967 — she was only 16! Francis Ford Coppola decided to turn the book into a film after he received a letter from a middle-school class. In 2005, he re-released the film including scenes that had been cut from the original — he wanted the new version to be closer to the book.

Quick Fact

An outsider is someone who is not accepted by a group or society.

Even though he is a member of the Greasers, Ponyboy still considers himself an "outsider." What qualities make people feel like they do not fit in?

Keith "Two-Bit" Mathews (Emilio Estevez)

Sodapop Curtis (Rob Lowe)

Ponyboy Curtis (C. Thomas Howell)

Dallas "Dally" Winston (Matt Dillon)

Darrel "Darry" Curtis (Patrick Swayze)

Johnny Cade (Ralph Macchio)

Steve Randle (Tom Cruise)

Quick Fact

It just doesn't make sense! *The Outsiders'* author S.E. Hinton was given Ds by her high-school creative writing teacher.

The Expert Says...

"The teenage years are highly charged and overly emotional ones, a mindset that S.E. Hinton (and by extension, director Francis Ford Coppola) captured perfectly."

— Preston Jones, journalist

The Last Laugh

This article tells the amazing story of how *The Outsiders* made it to the big screen.

Francis Ford Coppola was down in the dumps in 1982 when he got the letter from the librarian at Lone Star Junior High School. Despite winning five Oscars, his studio was bankrupt and he was outside "the winner's circle."

The librarian wrote that the students wanted him to make a movie of their favorite book, *The Outsiders*. She enclosed the book and the students' petition.

"It was signed by 110 little signatures," Coppola recalled. "Who can ignore that?"

It was a gamble that required a large cast. Coppola filmed with "outsider unknowns." Many critics hated it, but the kids, the cast of unknowns, and Coppola had the last laugh.

Coppola had an eye for talent and also recognized that the students were onto something. *The Outsiders* is a captivating story and great stories make movies. Recently, after Coppola's granddaughter asked him to show the movie to her class, he added more footage and re-released *The Outsiders*. After all, students were still requesting the movie of their favorite book!

BEFORE THEY WERE STARS

Back in 1983, the cast of *The Outsiders* was a bunch of not-so-famous young actors. Fast-forward to the present day and check out this list of the major films and TV shows for which these unknowns are now known.

Tom Cruise: *War of the Worlds* (2005), *Mission: Impossible III* (2006)

Matt Dillon: *Herbie Fully Loaded* (2005), *You, Me and Dupree* (2006)

Emilio Estevez: *The Mighty Ducks* (1992), *Bobby* (2006)

Diane Lane: *Under the Tuscan Sun* (2003), *Must Love Dogs* (2005)

Rob Lowe: *The West Wing* (TV) (1999 – 2006)

Ralph Macchio: *The Karate Kid* (1984)

Patrick Swayze: *Dirty Dancing* (1987), *Ghost* (1990)

Quick Fact

More than 12 million copies of *The Outsiders* novel have been sold!

Take Note

The fun of seeing an all-star cast when they were newbies earns *The Outsiders* our recognition. But is star quality enough? *The Outsiders'* plot is less confusing than *Crouching Tiger, Hidden Dragon*.

- Do you think that the plot of *The Outsiders* is more relevant than that of *Crouching Tiger*? Why or why not?

All's fair in love and war: Robin Wright Penn as Buttercup and Cary Elwes as Westley

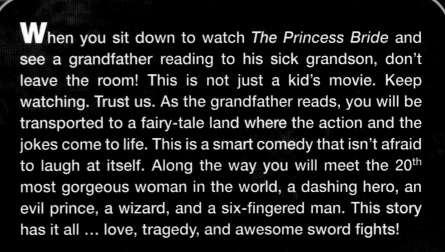

BRIDE

WHEN: This movie was released in 1987.

BASED ON: *The Princess Bride: S. Morgenstern's Classic Tale of Love and High Adventure,* by S. Morgenstern, abridged by William Goldman (1973)

WHY IT'S COOL: You can't go wrong with this combination of adventure, comedy, action, and romance (but watch out — this is a fairy tale with an edge).

When you sit down to watch *The Princess Bride* and see a grandfather reading to his sick grandson, don't leave the room! This is not just a kid's movie. Keep watching. Trust us. As the grandfather reads, you will be transported to a fairy-tale land where the action and the jokes come to life. This is a smart comedy that isn't afraid to laugh at itself. Along the way you will meet the 20th most gorgeous woman in the world, a dashing hero, an evil prince, a wizard, and a six-fingered man. This story has it all … love, tragedy, and awesome sword fights!

Turn the page to see why this movie, and the mysterious book that it is adapted from, made it into the #8 slot on our list.

THE PRINCESS BRIDE

WHAT'S THE STORY?

Buttercup is the most beautiful girl in the land, but her one true love, a stableboy named Westley, is too broke to marry her. Westley sails off to earn some cash, but soon after, Buttercup hears news that he's been killed. She vows never to love another — but ends up being forced to marry the evil Prince Humperdinck. The plot thickens. Before the wedding date, Buttercup is kidnapped! A masked rescuer is in hot pursuit. Will Buttercup escape from the kidnappers and be reunited with her one true love? Or will she be forced to marry Humperdinck?

CONFLICT ZONE

As soon as the swords are drawn, it becomes clear that this is definitely a good-versus-evil kind of movie.

? What are the main qualities of a fairy tale? Does this film have them?

FROM PAGE TO SCREEN

One of his daughters wanted a story about a princess, the other wanted a story about a bride, so what did writer William Goldman do? He combined the two ideas by writing *The Princess Bride* (published in 1973). Goldman was already a famous screenwriter when he wrote the book, so naturally, he also wrote the film's screenplay.

Quick Fact

When it was released, *The Princess Bride* didn't get much hype, but it did get an Oscar nomination for its theme song, "Storybook Love." When the movie came out on video, it gained popularity and now has a huge following of loyal fans.

The Expert Says...

"Children can see [*The Princess Bride*] as a bright, frothy adventure while adults will appreciate the subtlety and the sheer wit.

— William Gallagher, film critic

The Morgenstern Mystery

Put on your detective hat and read this article to find out who wrote *The Princess Bride!*

What does the *Itchy & Scratchy Show* have to do with *The Princess Bride*? Well, it's a bit of a stretch, but they are both stories within stories. Many think that the author of *The Princess Bride* book is a true genius for using this clever trick to tell the story, but others call him a liar. Which brings us to the question: who actually wrote *The Princess Bride*?

It would make sense to check the book cover, but it's not that easy: *The Princess Bride: S. Morgenstern's Classic Tale of True Love and High Adventure, The "Good Parts" Version,* abridged by William Goldman. As Goldman explains in the book's introduction: "Anyway, here's the 'good parts' version. S. Morgenstern wrote it. And my father read it to me. And now I give it to you." Goldman also tells us that he has cut out all of the boring historical stuff. Throughout the book, the reader is reminded that Goldman has edited the story because he includes entertaining comments about what is happening.

If you do some digging you will find out that this S. Morgenstern person has even written another book — so he must be real, right? NO! S. Morgenstern never existed. He was created by William Goldman (who eventually admitted this). When the book was turned into a movie, Goldman also wrote the script. The story within the story is told through a grandfather reading "Morgenstern's" tale to his grandson.

> **?** Why do you think a writer would use this technique?

Although some readers were upset that they were deceived, most of them enjoyed the story too much to stay mad. Goldman's creative storytelling is just one of the many reasons this has become one of the best-loved books (and films) of all time.

Quick Fact

To do the sword-fighting scenes, the actors practiced for hours on end and learned to fence with both their right and left hands. The result was one of the best fencing scenes ever filmed!

Take Note

Like *Crouching Tiger*, this movie has a romantic outlaw hero in pursuit of a fair maiden, and it also has lots of swordplay and action. But, this movie is a lot funnier! We think the laughs earn it the #8 slot.
- How important is humor when considering your favorite films? Explain.

5   4   3   2   1

When this film was made, computer-generated special effects were not an option. Instead, filmmakers used a mechanical shark and footage of a live great white.

WHEN: *Jaws* attacked theaters on June 20, 1975.

BASED ON: *Jaws,* by Peter Benchley (1974)

WHY IT'S COOL: *Jaws* is ONE SCARY MOVIE! But it's not your typical thriller — it introduced a new type of villain to the world.

Da-DUM ... da-DUM ... da-DUM, da-DUM, da-DUM ...

Quick, what do you think of when you hear that music? Does the hair on the back of your neck stand up? Of course!

Even though Peter Benchley's novel didn't have the benefit of the scary soundtrack, it still made a big enough splash on the best-seller list to catch the eye of a young and not-yet-famous director named Steven Spielberg. His creative genius helped to turn this page-turner into a film that changed movie history and terrorized generations of moviegoers.

From the first suspenseful scene to the explosive ending, viewers were on the edge of their seats in anticipation and horror. *Jaws* comes in at #7 on our list because it left its teeth marks on our society by changing the way we see the world: does anyone, anywhere, ever dip their toe in the ocean without wondering if Jaws is out there waiting to attack?

? Why do you think this movie had such a powerful effect on people?

JAWS

WHAT'S THE STORY?

A girl is eaten alive by a vicious shark at a peaceful New England beach. Police Chief Martin Brody tries to close the beach, but the town's mayor doesn't want to lose the tourism. The shark then helps himself to a few more swimmers and the hunt is on. But this isn't just any shark — this one's a giant great white with a big appetite and a nasty personality!

The police chief teams up with a young marine scientist, Hooper, and a grizzled shark hunter, Quint. The trio board the *Orca* for a "fishing trip" that becomes a heart-stopping struggle for survival.

CONFLICT ZONE

It is person against nature in this classic conflict with an almost legendary beast. While we bite our nails, Chief Brody must confront his very worst fears!

? What other person-versus-beast movies can you think of?

FROM PAGE TO SCREEN

Peter Benchley became a famous writer thanks to the publication of his novel *Jaws*, in 1974. With the 44-week best seller under his belt, Benchley and co-writers created the script for the *Jaws* movie. Then Spielberg's magic touch transformed it into this unforgettable thriller!

Police Chief Martin Brody tries to escape.

Quick Fact

The mechanical shark used in the movie broke down so often that Spielberg shot several scenes from the shark's point of view. This ended up making the film even scarier!

The Expert Says...

"One of the greatest horror films made. The opening sequence is not only a classic, it's still frightening nearly three decades after it was made.

— Forrest Hartman, film critic

7

10   **9**   **8**   **7**   **6**

BUSTED!

The popular TV show *MythBusters* was brave enough to test some famous scenes from *Jaws* to see if they could have happened in real life. Yes, they even used real great white sharks! Check out the results in this checklist …

Can a great white smash into and slice through a boat? **YES**

Will punching a shark in the nose or gills drive it away? **POSSIBLY**

Can a great white break through a shark cage? **YES**

Is a great white able to tow a large boat? **NO**

SCARED SILLY

Find out the secret of this film's success in this descriptive account.

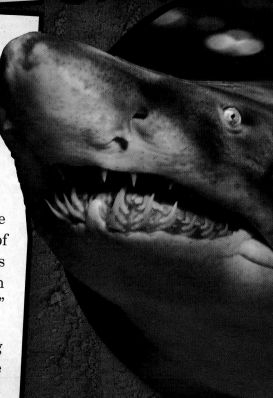

Every scary movie needs a few good jokes to ease the tension — and *Jaws* has them. One moment we're aboard *Orca*, singing along with the crew. The next, the water-level camera gives us the shark's perspective of the boat and our stomachs tighten. We gasp when Jaws first rises from the water, but burst out laughing when Brody tells Quint, "You're going to need a bigger boat!"

When the movie was first released, Steven Spielberg snuck into the back of theaters to watch the audience bouncing from laughter to screams in one breath. It's that delicate blend of terror and dark humor that makes *Jaws* a classic.

Quick Fact

Want to know all the gory details about this silver-screen shark? Ask your librarian or teacher for *The 10 Vilest Movie Villains*.

Take Note

Jaws has clamped down on the #7 spot on our list! Like *The Princess Bride* it makes us laugh; but then it makes us gasp. And we remember it every time we hit the beach!
• Do you agree with its position on our list? Go ahead — try to argue with Jaws.

5   4   3   2   1

Dance, dance: Keira Knightley as Elizabeth Bennet and Matthew Macfadyen as Mr. Darcy

EJUDICE

WHEN: Director Joe Wright gave us his take on this classic in 2005.

BASED ON: *Pride and Prejudice,* by Jane Austen (1813)

WHY IT'S COOL: Written by Jane Austen, *Pride and Prejudice* is considered by many to be the greatest love story ever written. Period.

Before you dismiss this as a boring film based on some dusty old novel from another century, read on. *Pride and Prejudice* is an energetic tale of the five beautiful and charming Bennet sisters. The lead role of Elizabeth is played by Keira Knightley — in the part that made her a star!

Pride and Prejudice is based on the boy-meets-girl, girl-hates-boy, but boy-loves-girl story line. A quote from the novel says it all: "We are all fools in love." And if you don't buy that line, there's plenty of stuff to keep you entertained — the humor, the costumes, the dances, and the complications of romantic relationships. Director Joe Wright, who was only 33 years old when he filmed this adaptation, has given this film a more youthful feel than other Jane Austen adaptations. And if that isn't enough reason to watch, there are scenes of the beautiful English countryside and talented actors!

 How might one's pride or prejudice interfere with a friendship or a relationship? What makes a good relationship?

PRIDE AND PREJUDICE

WHAT'S THE STORY?

Mrs. Bennet is afraid that her five daughters won't find suitable husbands to take care of them before their father dies. Imagine her excitement when two rich, handsome, and available men gallop into town.

Bachelor number one, Mr. Bingley, falls for Jane Bennet. Bachelor number two, Mr. Darcy, makes an insulting remark about her sister Elizabeth: "She isn't pretty enough to dance with." Jane is shy, so Bingley does not know she's also smitten with him. Bingley's sisters think Jane is not the right choice — her family is not wealthy enough. And Elizabeth wouldn't marry Darcy even if he were the last man on Earth. Or would she? Welcome to the complicated game of love!

CONFLICT ZONE

This film is definitely an example of opposites attract. The proud Darcy and the stubborn Elizabeth argue with each other despite the feelings they share. Who will win the battle?

FROM PAGE TO SCREEN

Jane Austen's *Pride and Prejudice*, published in 1813, is one of the most beloved novels ever written. It led the way for the modern romantic comedy. It was originally published anonymously because in those days it wasn't considered "proper" for women to write books.

Jane Austen (1775 – 1817) is known for her close observations of people and life in a small town. She writes with wit and irony about the snobbish society of her day. In a journal entry in 1826, Scottish poet and writer Sir Walter Scott wrote: "The young lady had a talent for describing feelings and characters of ordinary life ... [with an] exquisite touch, which renders ordinary commonplace things and characters interesting."

exquisite: *delicate and beautiful*
renders: *makes*

Quick Fact

In 2005, Keira Knightley was nominated for an Oscar for her portrayal of Elizabeth Bennet.

Actor Donald Sutherland as Mr. Bennet with four of his daughters

10 **9** **8** **7** **6**

TOUGH LOVE

You know the story well: Guy meets girl, guy and girl like each other, but some misunderstanding keeps them from getting together until the end of the story/movie. This isn't just the plotline of *Pride and Prejudice*, but it is the idea behind most romantic comedies.

Remember how Mr. Darcy (bachelor number two) said Elizabeth wasn't pretty enough to dance with? Check out this book excerpt where he starts to change his mind …

Quick Fact

Pride and Prejudice was nominated for four Oscars and over 35 international awards. It has grossed $120 million worldwide.

? Jane Austen's writing style is different from modern prose, but the characters in her novels are just as real for us now, 200 years after it was written. What does this extract tell you about the characters of Mr. Darcy and Elizabeth and their relationship?

Mr. Darcy had at first scarcely allowed her to be pretty; he had looked at her without admiration at the ball; and when they next met, he looked at her only to criticize. But no sooner had he made it clear to himself and his friends that she hardly had a good feature in her face, than he began to find it was rendered uncommonly intelligent by the beautiful expression of her dark eyes. …

He was forced to acknowledge her figure to be light and pleasing; and in spite of his asserting that her manners were not those of the fashionable world, he was caught by their easy playfulness. Of this she was perfectly unaware; to her he was only the man who made himself agreeable nowhere, and who had not thought her handsome enough to dance with.

He began to wish to know more of her …

scarcely: *almost not at all; barely*

The Expert Says…

" *Pride and Prejudice* combines sparkling writing, strong acting, exquisite settings, and passionate chemistry between Lizzie and Darcy in a brilliant adaptation of this beloved book. "

— Layla Voll, film critic

Take Note

Pride and Prejudice is the romance to end all romances — which is just so much more meaningful than the nightmares that *Jaws* gives us!
• Why do you think love stories are so popular? Are there other romance movies you like better? Remember, to make our list, they must originate from books.

5 4 3 2 1

(5) SHREK

The green giant, his donkey sidekick, and Princess Fiona

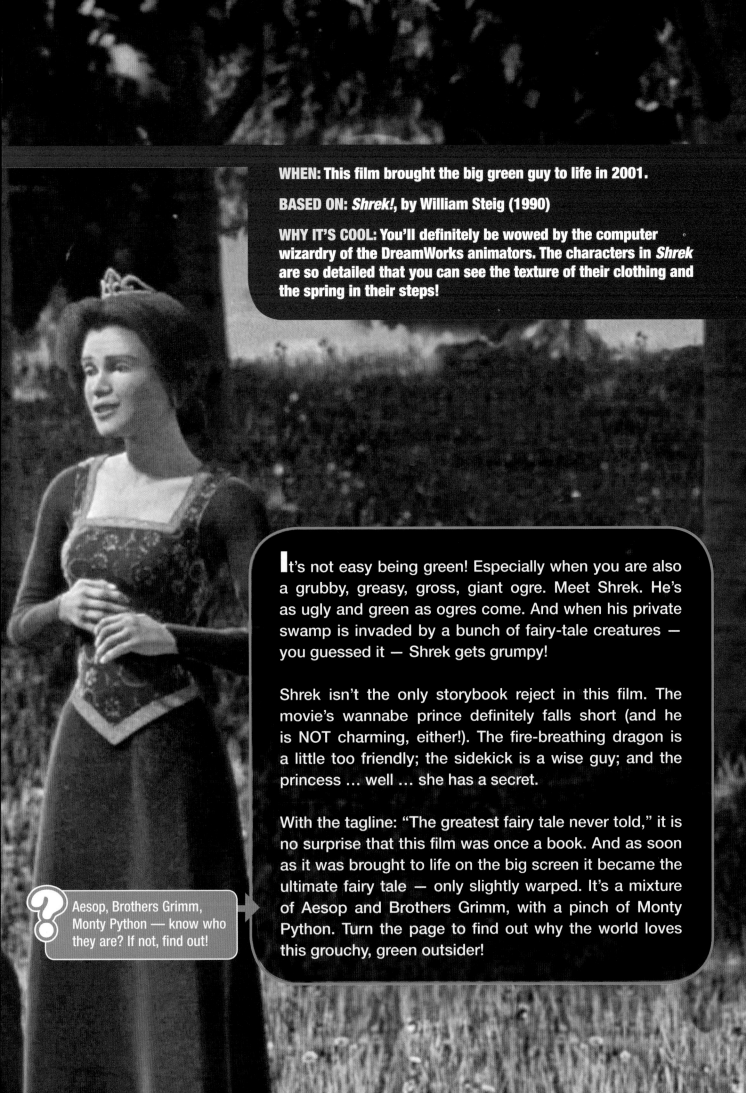

WHEN: This film brought the big green guy to life in 2001.

BASED ON: *Shrek!*, by William Steig (1990)

WHY IT'S COOL: You'll definitely be wowed by the computer wizardry of the DreamWorks animators. The characters in *Shrek* are so detailed that you can see the texture of their clothing and the spring in their steps!

It's not easy being green! Especially when you are also a grubby, greasy, gross, giant ogre. Meet Shrek. He's as ugly and green as ogres come. And when his private swamp is invaded by a bunch of fairy-tale creatures — you guessed it — Shrek gets grumpy!

Shrek isn't the only storybook reject in this film. The movie's wannabe prince definitely falls short (and he is NOT charming, either!). The fire-breathing dragon is a little too friendly; the sidekick is a wise guy; and the princess ... well ... she has a secret.

With the tagline: "The greatest fairy tale never told," it is no surprise that this film was once a book. And as soon as it was brought to life on the big screen it became the ultimate fairy tale — only slightly warped. It's a mixture of Aesop and Brothers Grimm, with a pinch of Monty Python. Turn the page to find out why the world loves this grouchy, green outsider!

? Aesop, Brothers Grimm, Monty Python — know who they are? If not, find out!

SHREK

WHAT'S THE STORY?

After his swamp is invaded by exiled fairy-tale creatures, Shrek travels to Duloc, to the tall mansion of the short ruler, Lord Farquaad. Shrek tries to convince Farquaad to allow the fairy-tale creatures to move back into their homes (and out of his swamp!). The cowardly Farquaad agrees, on one condition: Shrek must rescue Princess Fiona from the clutches of a fire-breathing dragon so that Farquaad can marry her and become king.

Quick Fact

Shrek! author William Steig wrote and drew until he was well into his 90s. During his career, he published over 30 children's books and more than 1,600 cartoons. No wonder he was known as the "King of Cartoons."

CONFLICT ZONE

In this twisted tale, things are not what they seem. This person-versus-ogre struggle might be a battle between good and evil, but there's also role reversal.

FROM PAGE TO SCREEN

This grown-up fairy tale is from a short book called *Shrek!*, by popular children's author and artist William Steig. The book won a School Library Journal award for Best Book of the Year in 1990. The storybook ogre is far uglier and scarier than the movie version.

Quick Fact

Bravo network gave *Shrek* the #3 slot on its list of the 100 Funniest Movies.

Do you agree that *Shrek* should be near the top of the list of funniest movies? Why or why not? Make your own list of the 10 Funniest Movies.

Shrek's "lady" friend tells him she's not into PDAs.

The Expert Says...

"Jolly and wicked, filled with sly in-jokes, and yet somehow possessing a heart."

— Roger Ebert, film critic

10 **9** **8** **7** **6**

He's Green and Groovy, Baby

A magazine article from *TV Guide Insider*, May 18, 2001

By Jeanne Wolf

Mike Myers, the funnyman — who supplies the not-so-jolly green giant's voice in the animated send-up of classic fairy tales — admits he borrowed heavily from the gluttonous Scotsman he created for *Austin Powers*. Why, you ask?

"At first, I was making Shrek sound Canadian," he says, "and I wasn't totally happy. Then I remembered that my mom, who's from Liverpool, used to read me children's stories with a British accent. And even though we had [already] recorded a lot of stuff, I said to the producers, 'I want to try something new.' So I made Shrek sort of British and Scottish." …

Myers clearly doesn't take the role too seriously. "I was worried about typecasting," he deadpans. "I think I've played too many green ogres." More thoughtfully, he offers, "I felt an affinity for Shrek, even though he's just an animated character. He's an outsider, he's misunderstood, and I related tremendously to that. When I was a kid, I was very small and I had acne. I think I felt left out and ignored just like Shrek did. That's why I love the message of the film, which is basically that you've got to learn to accept yourself for what you are."

Myers isn't worried that *Shrek* may go too far in its darkly humorous twisting of fairy tales … . "It's silly. It may be a little scary at times, but it's fun … I think kids will totally get it."

---

deadpans: *shows no emotion to make a joke funnier*
affinity: *feeling of closeness*

? This fairy tale has themes of forgiveness, loyalty, friendship, and inner beauty. Write down ways that people can learn to be less critical and more understanding of others.

Take Note

A superior example of the artistry of animation deserves recognition on any list of best movies, but fifth place means that *Shrek* is more than an excellent animated movie. It is an excellent animated movie that appeals to all ages.
• If you consider all the movies on our list so far, *Shrek* has something in common with each one of them. What are those common traits?

Quick Fact

In 2001, *Shrek* was the first movie to win an Oscar in the brand new category of Best Animated Feature.

5   4   3   2   1

Vivien Leigh as Scarlett O'Hara: The casual look was not too popular in 1939.

WIND

Gone With the Wind made cinematic history. Not only is it the highest-grossing movie of all time (when adjusted for inflation), but to this day, no other film has sold as many box office seats as it has!

Right from the start *Gone With the Wind* was surrounded by success. Published in 1936, Margaret Mitchell's book got rave reviews before the first copies even made it to the stores. Then the rights were sold to film producer David O. Selznick for $50,000 (the highest amount ever paid for movie rights at the time).

So why is a three-hour and 42-minute film about a bratty Southern belle such a smash hit? Why was it re-released with much acclaim in 1998? Why is it on more best-of lists than any other movie? Very simply, the movie tells a great story and tells it wonderfully.

It's about romance, survival, and the Civil War. A lot has changed since those days but the Technicolor glimpse that it gives of the Deep South during one of America's most troubled times remains a classic.

GONE WITH THE WIND

WHAT'S THE STORY?

Sassy Scarlett is upset. Her number one choice for a husband, Ashley, has ditched her to marry someone named Melanie. Then there's Rhett, whom Scarlett loves to hate. He finds this whole situation very funny (Rhett is played by Clark Gable — the Brad Pitt of his day!).

When the Civil War breaks out, Scarlett has other things to worry about. Her designer gowns are replaced by dresses made from drapery and her family is starving. Scarlett vows she'll "never be hungry again." But can she put her stubbornness to good use and save the home that she loves?

Quick Fact

Adjusted for inflation, *Gone With the Wind* would have earned $2,699,710,936 — more than any other film ever made! If you are talking about actual dollars earned, the movie *Titanic* tops the list with over $1.8 billion.

 Why is it important to compare the adjusted figures?

CONFLICT ZONE

The Yankees and the Confederates are fighting while Atlanta is burning. Scarlett is competing with Melanie for Ashley's affections, but the real struggle is the fight for survival in a country torn apart by war.

FROM PAGE TO SCREEN

Margaret Mitchell's friends thought she wasn't serious enough to write a novel. She proved them wrong with *Gone With the Wind* in 1936. Except for the Bible, *Gone With the Wind* has sold more copies than any other hardcover book. Take that, *Harry Potter*!

Quick Fact

Mail call! In 1990, Clark Gable as Rhett Butler and Vivien Leigh as Scarlett O'Hara were pictured on one of four 25¢ U.S. postage stamps honoring classic films.

The Expert Says...

"The ... saga of Scarlett O'Hara and Rhett Butler, played out against the flaming red backdrop of the Civil War, generates enough romance, historic drama, and deep emotion to fuel a dozen great films.

— Jack Garner, film critic

BEHIND THE SCENES

This Gone With the Wind timeline will blow your mind.

TAKE THIS JOB AND SHOVE IT!

In 1926, Margaret Mitchell is forced to quit her job because of arthritis. She spends most of her time reading in bed. After she has read all of the books in the library, her husband tells her she should write her own book.

A GENTLE BREEZE ...

The winds of inspiration start to blow as Mitchell decides to follow her husband's advice. It takes almost 10 years, but she writes *Gone With the Wind*, which is published on May 19, 1936.

HELLO HOLLYWOOD

In July 1936, movie producer David O. Selznick pays top dollar for the film rights to *Gone With the Wind*. It has already become a best-selling book.

YOU GO, GIRL!

Mitchell's novel wins the Pulitzer Prize for fiction on May 3, 1937. This prize is considered one of the highest achievements in American literary, journalistic, and musical fields.

THE A-LISTER OF 1938

Clark Gable signs for the role of Rhett Butler. His salary is $120,000.

arthritis: *disease that makes joints swollen and painful*

LIGHTS, CAMERA, ACTION!

Filming begins on December 10, 1938. After a year of hard work, the movie is finally completed in December 1939. The film's total budget was $4 million, making it the most expensive of its time.

ROLL OUT THE RED CARPET

On December 15, 1939, *Gone With the Wind* film premiere is held in Atlanta. Governor Rivers declares a three-day holiday and asks citizens to wear Civil War costumes.

OSCAR NIGHT

At the 12th annual Academy Awards, *Gone With the Wind* wins a record-breaking eight Oscars — including the first ever given to an African American, Hattie McDaniel (who played a slave in the film).

TRAGEDY

On August 11, 1949, Margaret Mitchell is hit by a drunk driver while crossing the street. Five days later she dies from her injuries.

Take Note

At #4, *Gone With the Wind* gets our nod as the all-time greatest romance. Watching the sparks fly between Vivien Leigh and Clark Gable is one of the best cinematic experiences ever (sorry, *Shrek*!). Speaking of cinematic, the movie's cinematography was groundbreaking and still endures several decades later.
- Romantics will argue that *Gone With the Wind* should be at the top of the list, or at least in the top three. If you are a romantic, state your case. If not, prepare to defend your choice!

Quick Fact

Over 33 million viewers tuned in when NBC aired *Gone With the Wind* in November 1976. It was the largest TV audience in history at that time.

5   **4**   3   2   1

Hermione (Emma Watson) casts a spell with Ron (Rupert Grint) and Harry Potter (Daniel Radcliffe).

ER

WHEN: Warner Brothers released the first *Harry Potter* movie (with a whole lot of hype) in 2001.

BASED ON: *Harry Potter and the Sorcerer's Stone,* by J.K. Rowling (1997)

WHY IT'S COOL: Even though the Harry Potter series was originally meant for young adults, the characters were so likable and the stories so original that people of all ages joined in on the Potter-mania.

Magic isn't just for witches and wizards anymore — Muggles (non-magical humans) can board the red train for Hogwarts and join in the adventure too. Whether you are 8 or 84, you will be enchanted by the charming heroes, nasty villains, and awesome magic in *Harry Potter and the Sorcerer's Stone*.

The story of this lonely orphan who's been neglected by his adopted family has won the hearts of millions of people all over the world. So much so that putting *Harry Potter and the Sorcerer's Stone* on the big screen was a definite no-brainer. When fans flocked to theaters to see their favorite characters in action, they weren't disappointed. And neither were we — and that's why this movie ranks #3 on our list …

HARRY POTTER

WHAT'S THE STORY?

On his 11th birthday, Harry Potter learns that he's a wizard. Like many British students, Harry goes off to boarding school — but it's no ordinary school. The lessons at Hogwarts School of Witchcraft and Wizardry include spells, transformations, and learning how to ride a magic broom. Harry makes friends with Ron and Hermione. But behind all of the fun, there's danger lurking … and you can be sure that Harry and his new friends will find it!

CONFLICT ZONE

The jagged lightning-bolt scar on Harry's forehead marks him as the only person to ever survive the killing power of the wicked wizard Voldemort. But Voldemort is back for revenge, and if Harry can't overcome his power, Voldemort will gain control of the whole wizard world!

FROM PAGE TO SCREEN

One of the great things about the movie is that most of the dialogue is lifted directly from the book. Author J.K. Rowling was very involved in the making of the film — she insisted that all the main actors had to be British.

? Why do you think J.K. Rowling wanted only British actors? Do you agree with her?

Quick Fact

Who needs a computer? J.K. Rowling wrote her first book by hand and then typed it on a secondhand typewriter.

Quick Fact

All seven books in the Harry Potter series will be made into movies. Check out how gangly child star Daniel Radcliffe, who plays Harry Potter, has matured into an adult as the series developed.

Now we're talking! The series has been translated into 55 languages — making it an around-the-world smash hit.

The Expert Says…

" It's eye-filling, well-cast, often very funny, and executed with great imagination and flair. "

— William Arnold, film critic

10　　**9**　　**8**　　**7**　　**6**

Do The Math

J.K. Rowling was on welfare while writing the first Harry Potter book. She even became upset because an editor who rejected her work didn't return her $7 manuscript folder. After many rejections, she thought she'd struck it rich when she got a $5,000 advance! The numbers are much better these days — just take a look at this fact chart!

$3,535,181,622:	The gross worldwide profit for all four of the movies
$976,475,550:	The worldwide box-office profits for the film
$100,000:	The approximate amount Scholastic paid for the U.S. publishing rights for *Sorcerer's Stone*
300 million:	The number of copies of Harry Potter books that have sold worldwide

All this totals up to a $4-billion empire, which gives Rowling a fortune of $1 billion. This earned her the 746th spot on the list of the richest people in the world in 2006! To put that into perspective, she's not as rich as Oprah at $1.4 billion, but she's richer than Queen Elizabeth at $500 million!

4:	The number of Harry Potter movies made so far (3 more on the way)
#3:	The film's rank on the list of all-time top-grossing movies world-wide (it's also the number of Oscar nominations the film received!)

? Do you think that a film's quality should be judged by the amount of money it makes or the number of awards it receives? Explain your answer.

5:	Video games based on the books and movies
Over 400:	Spin-off products made

Take Note

When it comes to special effects, this movie ranks very highly. When it comes to charm and likability, *Harry Potter* could top our list. Solidly grounded in a book that made the world believe in magic, the movie has that same universal appeal.

• What other films on this list have similar appeal? It is difficult to dispute success, and Harry Potter is an immensely popular phenomenon. *Harry Potter* has the world at its feet. Does it have you? Why?

5 4 **3** 2 1

Adding up the running time of the three extended-version DVDs makes this a 682-minute masterpiece!

RINGS TRILOGY

WHEN: *The Fellowship of the Ring* was released in 2001, *The Two Towers* in 2002, and *The Return of the King* in 2003.

BASED ON: *The Fellowship of the Ring* (1954), *The Two Towers* (1954), *The Return of the King* (1955), by J.R.R. Tolkien

WHY IT'S COOL: The best work of one of the most brilliant authors in history, plus the most complex cinematography ever attempted equals *magnum opus* (that's Latin for "a great work").

*T*he *Lord of the Rings* books push fantasy to the limit. With their enormous cast of characters, spectacular settings, supernatural creatures, epic battles, and gigantic scope, it seems that these books would be impossible to turn into film. Walt Disney owned the movie rights for 10 years, but didn't even try it. Several others thought about it, but gave up.

Then a director named Peter Jackson said he was up for the challenge of capturing one of the most popular works of literature on film. Re-creating J.R.R. Tolkien's epic story definitely wasn't easy. Many movie sets, costumes, and props had to be built twice (hobbit-sized and human-sized), highly detailed computer-generated effects had to be developed, and an army of cast and crew had to be assembled. The mammoth task demanded meticulous skill and artistry, attention to detail and, above all, organization! It took eight long years and went WAY over budget …

But Jackson did it — and Tolkien fans around the world have been thanking him ever since.

THE LORD OF THE RINGS TRILOGY

WHAT'S THE STORY?

If you can believe it, there's nonstop action in this nine-hour trilogy and it's all about the One Ring. The Dark Lord Sauron wants it so that he can have ultimate power. In *The Fellowship of the Ring*, the ring is given to a likable young hobbit named Frodo. Assisted by the Fellowship of the Ring he sets off on a mission to destroy it.

Then there's *The Two Towers* ... While the Fellowship makes new friends and fights other battles, Frodo and his sidekick, Sam, must continue to Mordor in their quest to destroy the ring.

The journey ends in *The Return of the King*. The Fellowship prepares to fight the final battle for Middle-earth while Frodo and Sam approach Mount Doom.

ultimate: *highest*

CONFLICT ZONE

It's classic good versus evil in this ambitious story. We learn that true courage doesn't mean never being afraid — it means having the strength to face your fears and keep on going.

FROM PAGE TO SCREEN

Publishers decided to release *The Lord of the Rings* in 1954 and 1955 over three volumes, so the first affordable book would capture the readers and maximize profit. The trilogy's success established J.R.R. Tolkien as the founder of modern fantasy. It's no surprise that the moviemakers used the same tactic with astounding success!

? What are some of the challenges of turning an incredibly long book into a film (or films?)

J.R.R. Tolkien (1892 – 1973) never thought that his fictional stories would become popular. In fact, it was his friend C.S. Lewis who persuaded him to publish *The Hobbit* in 1937.

Quick Fact

The three *The Lord of the Rings* movies were nominated for a total of 30 Academy Awards and won 17. *The Return of the King* won all 11 Oscars for which it was nominated, including Best Picture!

Left to right: Billy Boyd, Dominic Monaghan, Elijah Wood, and Sean Astin

10   9   8   7   6

PETER JACKSON SPEAKS ...

❝You make decisions as a filmmaker and, rightly or wrongly, you change things if you think they need to be changed.❞

An interview by Nina Rehfeld, December 18, 2002

Nina: Could you talk a bit about the changes you made to the book's original story this time? In the first one, you were very true to the book ...

Peter Jackson: Not really. It's an illusion! [laughs] No, no, you're right. I know what you mean.

Nina: In the book, for example, the character Faramir is very pure and very noble, but here in the film, he's got this evil touch. He's even tempted by the ring.

Peter Jackson: For a short time, yeah. We made that change, just to use that example — and this is really where being a filmmaker differs from being a writer. You make decisions as a filmmaker and, rightly or wrongly, you change things if you think they need to be changed. We wanted the episode with Faramir in this particular film to have a certain degree of tension. Frodo and Sam were captured. Their journey had become more complicated by the fact that they are prisoners. Which they are in the book for a brief period of time. But then, very quickly in the book, Tolkien sort of backs away from there and, as you say, he reveals Faramir to be very pure. At one point, Faramir says, "Look, I wouldn't even touch the ring if I saw it lying on the side of the road."

For us, as filmmakers, that sort of thing creates a bit of a problem because we've spent a lot of time in the last film and in this one to establish this ring as incredibly powerful. Then, to suddenly come to a character that says, "Oh, I'm not interested in that," to suddenly go against everything that we've established ourselves is sort of going against our own rules. ...

The reality is that *The Two Towers* is the slightest of the books, I think. We kind of have all the memorable moments of the book in the film and what we've done is to actually enhance and add bits of story that weren't in the book.

---

complicated: *made more difficult*
slightest: *least important*

Quick Fact

The Return of the King is the second-highest-grossing movie in history, with earnings of over $1.1 billion. The three films' combined box-office earnings add up to just under $3 billion.

The Expert Says ...

❝Will undoubtedly last through the decades as one of the most ambitious and mind-blowingly successful celluloid projects ever undertaken.**❞**

— Phil Villarreal, film critic

Take Note

Peter Jackson accomplished the most mammoth task ever attempted in movies. The scope and detail in this production are staggering. What makes *Rings* truly outstanding is the quality of the accomplishment.

• Although three of our other selections are visually stunning (can you name them?), *Rings* leaves them in its dust. It is well worth all of the awards it has won. We believe that only one movie from a book bests it. Can you predict #1?

5   **4**   **3**   **2**   **1**

Share the moment: Atticus Finch (played by Gregory Peck) and his daughter Scout (Mary Badham)

TO KILL A MOCKINGBIRD MOVIE STILL — BETTMANN/CORBIS

CKINGBIRD

WHEN: On December 25, 1962, Universal Pictures gave the world a special gift. *To Kill a Mockingbird* was released and it became a silver-screen classic!

BASED ON: *To Kill a Mockingbird,* by Harper Lee (1960)

WHY IT'S COOL: Gregory Peck won an Oscar for portraying Atticus Finch. The American Film Institute named Finch "the greatest movie hero of the 20th century." The film also helped kick-start the civil rights movement!

To Kill a Mockingbird changed history!

What more important thing can be said about either a movie or a book? It is one thing to amuse or entertain, and another to change the world. *To Kill a Mockingbird* definitely did both! The book and the movie possessed enough quality, endurance, and courage to change the way society thought and acted.

To Kill a Mockingbird tells the story with a great script and impressive acting. It does not rely on stunts or amazing special effects. The story line is simple — a father's struggle seen through the eyes of his 10-year-old son and his six-year-old daughter. But the idea behind the story is important because it is about taking a stand for what you believe in — even if that goes against what other people think.

Even though the movie wasn't expected to be a blockbuster, Universal Pictures (whose profits depended on audience approval) took a stand. They picked a fine actor to tell an important story and to teach the world that we, too, should stand up for what we believe in.

 Name a movie you have seen that deals with strong beliefs or values. How well did the acting add to the story?

TO KILL A MOCKINGBIRD

WHAT'S THE STORY?

Atticus Finch is a respected lawyer and an ideal father. But his son, Jem, and daughter, Scout, don't see him as quite so perfect. Along with their pal Dill, they are more interested in pestering the hermit next door — the scary Boo Radley.

But Atticus has more serious worries. While defending Tom Robinson, an African-American man wrongly accused of assaulting a white girl, Atticus must try to shield both his client and his children from the racial prejudice that exists so strongly in the society in which they live.

CONFLICT ZONE

Racism is the unquestioned way of life in Maycomb, Alabama, during the Great Depression. It's a "colored man" versus almost everyone else as Atticus Finch stands up to defend Tom from false accusations and prove his innocence.

FROM PAGE TO SCREEN

Both the movie and the book are considered to be classics. Controversial as it was in 1960, *To Kill a Mockingbird* won Harper Lee, a new writer, a Pulitzer Prize. A 1991 survey by the Library of Congress named the book second only to the Bible in being most often named as making a difference in people's lives.

prejudice: *unfair opinion, usually unfavorable*

Atticus teaches Scout not to judge until you have "stood in someone's shoes and walked around in them for a while." How can movies help us walk around in another person's shoes?

Gregory Peck as Atticus Finch

The Expert Says...

"*To Kill a Mockingbird* … is one of those rare productions where everything is in place — a superior script, a perfect cast, and a director who has a clear vision and achieves what he sets out to do. *To Kill a Mockingbird* is universally recognized as a classic, and the label is well deserved."

— James Berardinelli, film critic

Quick Fact

In the 1930s, nine African-American youths called The Scottsboro Boys were falsely accused and convicted of assaulting two white women. Their trials were an influence for the book.

10   **9**   **8**   **7**   **6**

THE MOCKINGBIRD STILL SINGS

For many teens, it's difficult to imagine the way things were back in the 1960s. But in the era of *To Kill a Mockingbird*, this list of facts shows that the world was a different place …

- In 1961, a group of students organized "freedom rides" in which they traveled by bus to try to desegregate bus terminals in the southern United States. One of the buses was firebombed, causing the riders to flee.

- On August 28, 1963, Martin Luther King, Jr.'s brave voice bellowed the famous words, "I have a dream."

- Only days after King's speech, African-American teens Cynthia Wesley, Carole Robertson, Addie Mae Collins, and Denise McNair were killed when their church was bombed.

- In 1964, James Chaney, Andrew Goodman, and Michael Schwerner (all in their early 20s) were murdered in Philadelphia, Mississippi, while campaigning to register African Americans to vote.

desegregate: *end racial separation*

In the commotion that followed these events, the persistent message of *To Kill a Mockingbird* taught people to stand up against prejudice. When you watch this film from a sofa at home or a desk at school, remember those people (of all races) who marched and struggled and believed that things could change.

Although it is a soft-spoken movie, *To Kill a Mockingbird* still manages to challenge the world and inspire people to change. In today's complex world, it still challenges moviemakers to use the power of film to speak courageously. In our lives, *To Kill a Mockingbird* still reminds us to stand up for what we believe in.

? List the qualities a film would need to be considered a classic. What qualities would make a book a classic?

Quick Fact

Talk about quitting while you're ahead! *To Kill a Mockingbird* is the only book that Harper Lee has ever written. When asked why she didn't write another novel, Lee said, "When you're at the top, there's only one way to go."

Take Note

To Kill a Mockingbird was carefully and wisely filmed in black and white. It did not need Technicolor cinematography to deal with what should be black and white. There is no gray area in the belief that all people are created equal. Gregory Peck is superb and he is supported by young actors who totally convince us with their honesty. This is a movie that took a risk and changed history. So we took a risk. We looked beyond all of the fancy filming techniques and elaborate plots and did what we considered "the right thing" and made this #1.

- We selected a quiet, thoughtful film as our best movie from a book. Does the *Mockingbird* still sing to you? Why or why not?

5   4   3   2   1

What Do You Think?

1. Do you agree with our ranking? If you don't, try ranking them yourself. Justify your ranking with data from your own research and reasoning. You may refer to our criteria, or you may want to draw up your own list of criteria.

2. Here are three other movies that we considered but in the end did not include in our top 10 list: *Forrest Gump*, *Jurassic Park*, and *Charlie and the Chocolate Factory*.
   - Find out more about them. Do you think they should have made our list? Give reasons for your response.
   - Are there other movies from books that you think should have made our list? Explain your choices.

Index